FUTURE WINGS

THE STEP-BY-STEP PAPER SPACECRAFT BOOK

WRITTEN BY SHARI COHEN & ILLUSTRATED BY NEAL YAMAMOTO

LOWELL HOUSE JUVENILE

LOS ANGELES

CONTEMPORARY BOOKS

CHICAGO

Publisher: Jack Artenstein
Director of Publishing Services: Rena Copperman
Executive Managing Editor, Lowell House Juvenile: Brenda Pope-Ostrow
Editor in Chief, Lowell House Juvenile: Amy Downing
Art Director: Lisa-Theresa Lenthall
Cover Photograph: Ann Bogart
Cover Craft: Charlene Olexiewicz

Lowell House books can be purchased at special discounts when ordered in bulk for premiums and special sales. Contact Department TC at the following address:

Lowell House Juvenile
2020 Avenue of the Stars, Suite 300
Los Angeles, CA 90067
Library of Congress Catalog Card Number is available.
ISBN: 1-56565-653-9
Manufactured in the United States of America

10 9 8 7 6 5 4 3 2 1

Contents

Before You Start

The exploration of space is an exciting adventure. Rockets have taken us around the world and to the moon. Satellites placed in orbit supply us with important scientific information, and space probes search the mysteries of the unknown.

Future Wings will show you how to be part of this adventure by making and designing your own spacecraft, many unlike anything that has been flown before.

From UFOs to blasting rockets, and even replicas of early spacecraft and shuttles, each design is challenging and fun to create.

For years scientists have been looking to the future, designing new space machines to explore the universe. Now you can, too!

MAKING YOUR DESIGN

Some projects in *Future Wings* are designed after existing spacecraft, such as *Explorer 1* and the *Saturn 5 Rocket.* Many others are original rockets that, for now, have only been built by kids like you! Who knows, maybe one day you'll be part of a team who creates some futuristic flying machines like those found in this book, to explore the edges of the universe and beyond.

The *Future Wings* designs you choose to make not only look different from each other, they will also fly in a variety of ways. Some will be direct fast fliers, some will loop and turn, and others will float softly to the ground after being launched.

A GOOD FLIGHT REQUIRES A GOOD LAUNCH

After you have completed your design, you will want to use the perfect launch to send it soaring. Here are five different launches that you can use for your *Future Wings* designs.

The Shoe Box Launch

1. You will need one shoe box (average size, 12″ x 6″) without the lid. Turn the box over so that the opening is on the bottom. Cut out a large rectangle in the top of the box, leaving about 1½″ on all sides. Cover the top with aluminum foil but leave the rectangle open. You can fold the extra foil around the edges of the rectangle.

2. Place a large rubber band over the whole box, widthwise, as shown. The rubber band should be snug but not too tight. The top part of the rubber band acts as a spring launch, similar to a slingshot. Set your rocket on the band and pull it and the rubber band deep into the box. Aim it upward and release.

   This launch works best with Explorer 1.

The Disc Launch

Hold the spacecraft in your hand as you would a Frisbee®. Toss it outward. If you are outside, throw it into the wind rather than against it.

This launch works best with the Ulysses Solar Satellite.

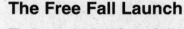

The Target Thrust Launch

The target thrust launch is a hard, fast overhand throw. Hold the craft above your shoulder and throw outward and slightly upward for a long-distance flight.

This launch works best with the Astro Blaster, *the* Imperial Attack, *the* Stage 1 Command Missile, *and the* Saturn 5 Rocket.

The Free Fall Launch

To launch the free fall designs, carefully stand at a high point such as the top of a balcony. Drop the craft, bottom pointed down, and it will either float or twirl toward the ground with the help of an upward air current.

This launch works best with the Global Storm Tracker *and* Time Trax.

The Straight Pitch Launch

The straight pitch launch is used on many of the *Future Wings* designs. It is a direct hand-throw aimed ahead of you and will help give your craft a fast, steady flight. Hold your craft above your shoulder and grip it securely using your thumb and forefinger. Push outward and slightly up for a faster flight.

This launch works best with the Space Shuttle, *the* Ramjet Rocket, *the* Unknown Visitor, *the* Jupiter 9 Space Probe, *the* Thermal Spy Glider, *the* Gamma Ray Observer, Thunder Flight, *the* Telstar Alien Search, *the* Silver Prowler, and *the* Rescue Rangers.

FINE-TUNING FOR A PERFECT FLIGHT

The same forces that allow gliders and kites to stay in the air apply to paper spacecraft as well. All objects are affected by such things as weight, force, and balance as they move through the air. Don't get discouraged if you don't get a perfect flight on the first throw. You might need to make some adjustments in the design. Remember to make your folds neat and crisp. You will discover which speeds and angles work best for you. Each design has an ideal flying angle, usually found by trial and error.

Below, you'll find some ideas to help you if you are having problems getting your spacecraft off the ground.

If it stalls in the air:

• Try folding down the back elevator flaps.

• Take off some of the tape or stickers. Too many decorations can add to the weight of your spacecraft.

If it takes a nosedive:

• Bend the wings up slightly and make sure that they are even. Some upward flaps may be needed along the back and wings.

• If there are paper clips on the nose tip of the craft, take one off.

If it takes a tail dive:

• Add weight to the nose with a paper clip.

• Try bending some elevator flaps down.

If it rolls:

• Adjust the back rudder. Turn the rudder toward the left if the craft tilts to the right, and turn the rudder toward the right if it tilts to the left.

• Make sure that your middle folds are crisp and even.

Now you have the tools and information for designing your own spacecraft. You can build a craft of your choice and, if you want, change the look using different colors and decorations. The ideas are limitless. When you have finished, you will have created an incredible collection of super space machines. Have a blast!

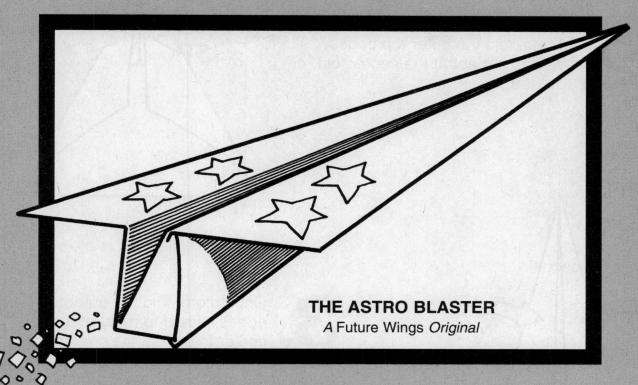

THE ASTRO BLASTER
A Future Wings *Original*

Falling meteoroids can travel through the earth's atmosphere and hit the ground, sometimes causing destruction. The *Astro Blaster*'s sleek design enables it to speed through the atmosphere to overtake and destroy a meteoroid, before it damages the earth's surface.

YOU NEED:

8½" x 11" piece of paper
3" square piece of paper
yellow and gold crayons
ruler
pencil

scissors
markers or stickers (optional)

1. Lay out your 8½" x 11" paper. Crease lengthwise. Open. Fold each top corner of the paper to meet at the center fold. Crease.

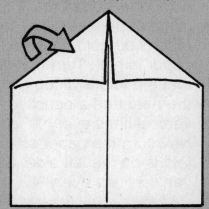

2. Again, fold the outer top edges inward to meet at the center fold. Crease.

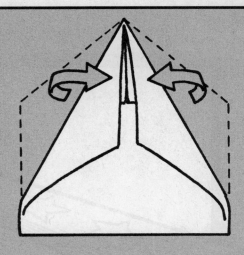

3. Once more, fold the outer top edges inward to meet at the center fold. Fold the craft in half, so that the folded edges are on the inside. Lay the craft in front of you with the point facing right. Take the frontmost wing and fold its top diagonal edge to the bottom flat edge. Turn the craft over (now the point is facing left) and repeat.

4. To make the engine sparks, first color one side of the 3″ square piece of paper yellow, then the other side gold. Fold the square paper in half. Turn the paper so that the fold is along the top. Use the ruler and a pencil to sketch vertical lines every ¼″ across it. Now turn the paper so that the fold is on the left side. Sketch vertical lines every ¼″.

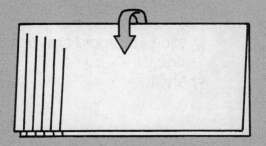

5.

Cut along the lines from the bottom, upward, creating several long, thin strips. Keep the fold line intact. Then cut along the horizontal lines to make many tiny squares.

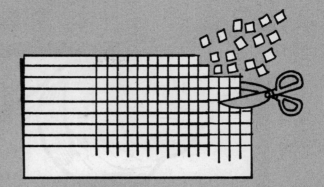

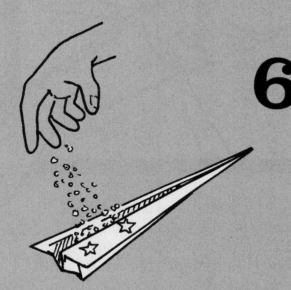

6.

Gather the squares and sprinkle them along the top opening of the *Astro Blaster* rocket. Pinch the rocket closed by holding it at the bottom. Decorate with stars, or as desired.

TO FLY: Use the target thrust launch. Grasp the underside of the rocket and throw upward. As your rocket soars into the air, the engine sparks fly**!**

AMAZING FACTOID!

Meteoroids are pieces of matter that move through outer space and enter the earth's atmosphere to form meteors. These meteors usually fall apart in flight and fall to earth as dust. The meteors that reach the earth's surface before they are completely consumed or vaporized are called meteorites. The largest known meteorite is estimated to weigh about 55 tons!

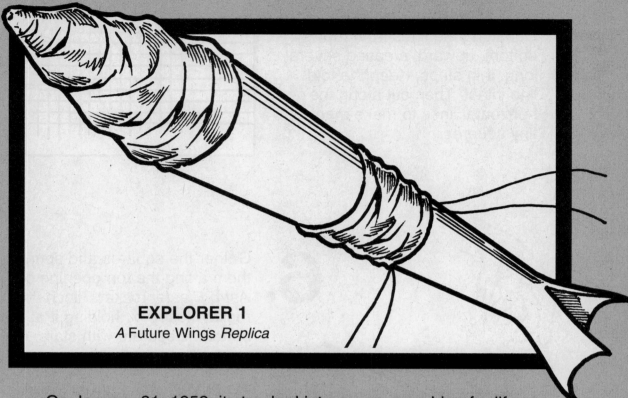

EXPLORER 1
A Future Wings *Replica*

On January 31, 1958, it streaked into space searching for life on other planets of the solar system. It was called *Explorer 1,* and it was America's first robot in space.

Like a spy in the sky, this pencil-shaped satellite flew over 1,500 miles above the earth's atmosphere, taking measurements of radiation, heat, light, and magnetic fields.

YOU NEED:

8½″ x 11″ piece of paper
ruler
tape
two pieces of foil, 5″ square
    and 4″ x ½″

scissors
two 12″ pieces of thread
pencil

1. To make the body of the rocket, roll the 8½″ x 11″ paper lengthwise into a long tube. The width of the opening should be ¾″. Tape along the seam to secure.

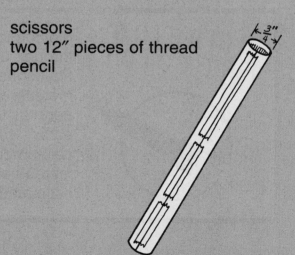

2. To make the nose section, take the 5″ square of foil and roll it around three or four fingers. Tape the seam.

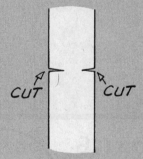

3. Shape the top of the foil into a point and slide the nose section over one end of the body. Place tape around the bottom of the nose section to hold it secure to the body.

4. At the middle section of the body, cut two slits on each side as shown. Make sure not to cut all the way through the body.

CUT   CUT

5. To add the four radio antennae (thread), bend the body of the rocket slightly until you can see all the way through the middle cut. Now slip the two pieces of thread through each slit as seen in the diagram.

6. Wrap the 4″ x ½″ strip of foil tightly around the middle of the rocket, covering the two side cuts. Tape to close. The two pieces of thread will hang loose on each side of the rocket.

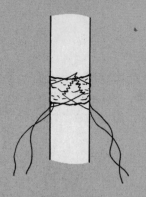

7. Sketch a light line 2″ from the bottom of the rocket upward. Cut along this line, going through both sides and making two bottom flaps.

8. Grasp both flaps and bend outward as shown.

AMAZING FACTOID!

The body of *Explorer 1* was originally covered with tiny solar cells that converted sunlight to electricity. This was later changed to the windmill-like solar panels that are found on many buildings today.

TO FLY: Use the shoe box launch. Place each bottom flap on one side of the top rubber band. Pull rocket deep down into the box, aim, and release. The rocket will shoot upward at a fast speed.

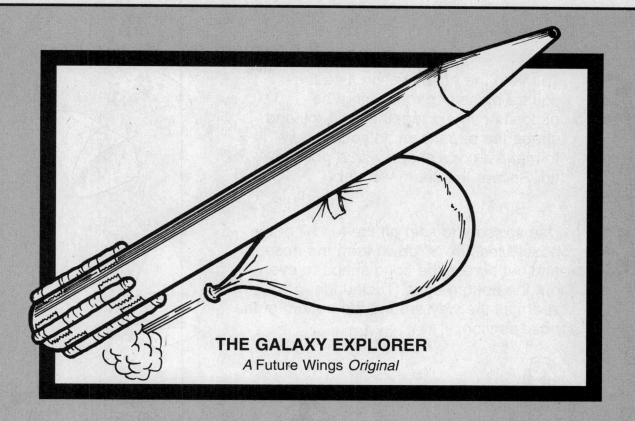

THE GALAXY EXPLORER
*A Future Wings *Original

The *Galaxy Explorer* is a space cruiser that flies to the stars. Standing over 200 feet high, it is lifted out of the earth's orbit and sent into deep space.

The *Explorer* carries a crew of 10 astronauts who live and work on the spaceship for one year, gathering scientific information from various stars to share with the world.

YOU NEED:

8½″ x 11″ piece of paper	glue
tape	three 4″ drinking straw pieces
ruler	foil
4″ square piece of paper	thread, 10′ long
scissors	balloon

1. Roll the 8½″ x 11″ piece of paper into a long tube and secure it with tape. The diameter or width of the tube should measure ¾″ wide.

2. To make the nose section, use the 4″ square piece of paper. Bring the opposite corners together and roll and shape the paper around your fingers to make a cone shape with a pointed tip. Secure the seam with tape.

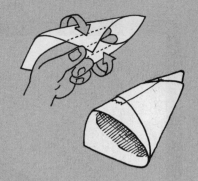

3. Use scissors to snip off the top ¼″ of the nose. Measure 3″ down from the nose tip and cut across the cone shape to even out the bottom edge. Tuck under a ½″ seam all the way around the bottom of the nose section.

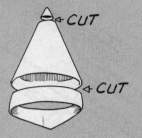

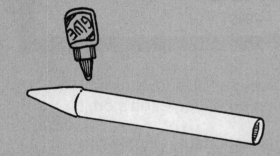

4. Dot glue in a ring around the top edge of the body of the rocket. Slide the nose section tightly over the top and let the glue dry for five minutes.

5. Take the three straw pieces and cover each with foil. These are your fuel tanks. Place a line of glue along one side of each tank. Tape the tanks around the bottom of the rocket. Let glue set for five minutes.

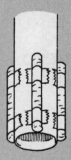

Investigate!

When you launch this craft, notice how fast the balloon travels as the air leaves it. The *Galaxy Explorer* is launched by releasing compressed air from the balloon. The air is a gas, much like the fast-burning fuel that actual rockets burn, which pushes out the pressurized air and moves it ahead.

6. Drop one end of the thread through the whole body of the rocket, including the nose section. If needed, wet the end of the thread to make it easier to slide through.

7. Tie one end of the thread to a low point near the floor, such as a chair leg. Tie the other end of the thread to a higher point in the room—a bedpost, for instance. Make sure the thread is pulled tight and straight.

8. Blow up the balloon as much as you can. Keeping the air hole pinched tight, tape the balloon to the middle section of the rocket.

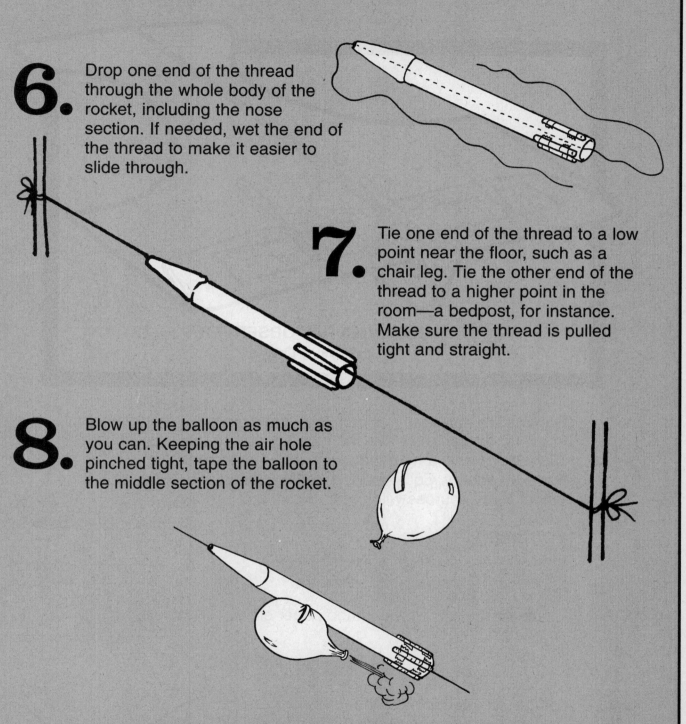

TO FLY: Hold the balloon (with rocket attached) at the low point on the thread. Release your fingers from the balloon and it will shoot ahead, carrying the rocket to the top of the thread.

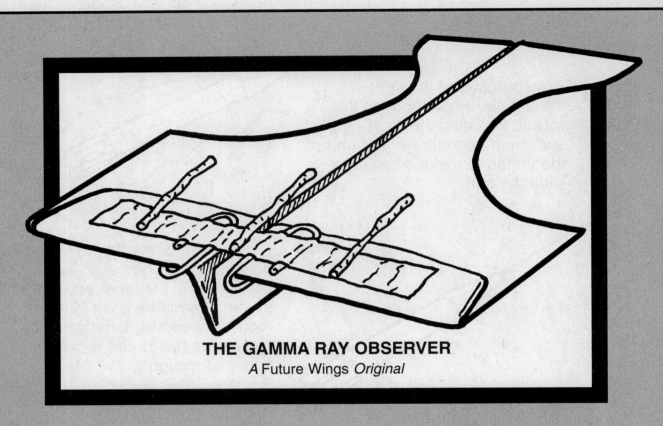

THE GAMMA RAY OBSERVER
A Future Wings Original

Gamma rays are a mysterious high-energy source that bounce from star to star and travel with the speed of light. The *Gamma Ray Observer* is a manned spacecraft that studies this powerful energy. Equipped with three moving telescopes, it can detect X-ray sources within our galaxy and beyond.

YOU NEED:

ruler
pencil
8½″ x 11″ piece of paper
scissors

four foil pieces, one 4″ x 1″ and three 2″ x ½″
tape
two jumbo paper clips

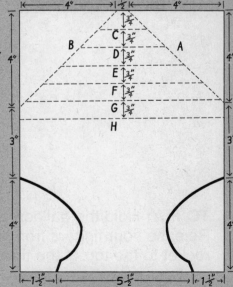

1.

Using the dimensions at the right, use a ruler and pencil to copy the design onto an 8½″ x 11″ sheet of paper.

2. Cut out along the two dark solid lines shown in Step 1. Fold under at lines A and B.

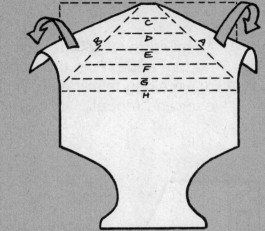

3. Take the top point and fold down along line C. Fold again on line D; then fold again on line E, line F, line G, and finally, line H.

4. Turn design so that the widest flat side is facing to the left. Fold in half, bringing the bottom side to meet the top side. Make sure your folds are crisp and even.

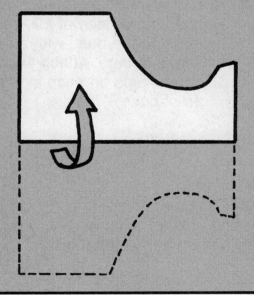

5. Lightly draw a ½″ line along the bottom edge. Fold the front wing down along this line. Turn craft over and repeat.

6. Fold the 4″ x 1″ piece of foil in half. Place evenly over the front end of the *Observer* as shown. Tape each end to hold in place.

7. To make the telescopes, roll the three 2″ x ½″ foil strips into long cylinders. Place each strip across the larger piece of foil, securing each to the base with a small piece of tape. Attach two jumbo paper clips on each side of the front nose.

TO FLY: Use the straight pitch launch, tossing upward and out. The *Gamma Ray Observer* is a great glider.

AMAZING FACTOID!

When were the first gamma rays discovered? They were first detected in 1972, using equipment aboard a U.S. *OSO-3* satellite.

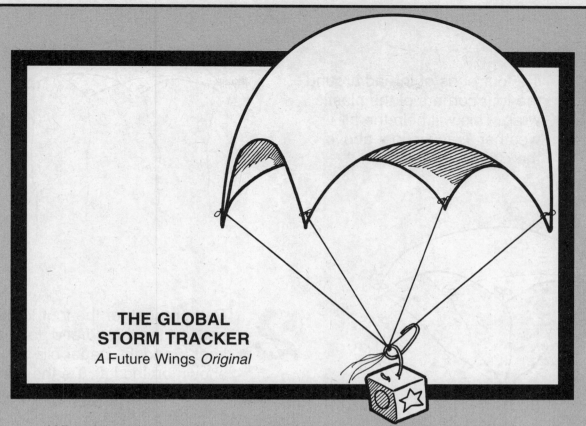

**THE GLOBAL
STORM TRACKER**
A Future Wings *Original*

When severe thunder and lightning are in the forecast, the
Global Storm Tracker is launched from a rocket and released
high above the threatening clouds. It gathers information about
weather problems, and it can help predict hurricanes and
tornadoes.

   Inside the *Tracker* is a small radio transmitter. It relays data
about the wind and humidity surrounding a storm to receiving
stations on the ground and to ships at sea.

YOU NEED:

four 12″ strands of thread
10″ x 10″ piece of clear
   plastic wrap
small paper clip
4″ x 3″ piece of paper

pencil
stickers and markers for
   decoration
scissors
tape

1. Tie four ends of thread around the four corners of the plastic wrap. This will help the all-weather *Tracker* float above the clouds.

2. Gather together the four loose ends of the thread and tie in a knot. Bend the paper clip as shown on the left. Tie the end thread pieces through the loop and double-knot.

3. Using the 4″ x 3″ piece of paper, trace over the design at the right including the fold lines. If you want to decorate your *Global Storm Tracker,* color the design now. Cut out design and crease at lines marked "fold."

FOLD

FOLD

FOLD

FOLD

FOLD

FOLD

FOLD

FOLD

4. Fold the design into a perfect square shape by joining together the edges. Before you tape the edges, poke two tiny holes in the square. This is where you will attach the paper clip. Hold the edges of the design and tape to close into a cube.

5. Slip the paper clip into the two holes like a hook. The *Global Storm Tracker* can be spotted by approaching spacecraft or high-flying planes.

TO FLY: Use the free fall launch. Billow out the *Tracker,* then drop it from a high spot in the room or an outdoor balcony. The craft will float through the air on its way down. **Make sure you choose a safe and sturdy place to stand before you launch your spacecraft.**

Investigate!

How does the *Global Storm Tracker* float through the air after it is launched? As the parachute falls, air is trapped inside it. The air pushes upward and keeps the parachute from crashing to the ground.

To see the force of air on objects, take two pieces of paper. Roll one piece into a ball. Keep the other piece flat. From a high place like a chair, drop the rolled paper ball down. Now drop the flat piece of paper. Which took the longest to drop? The flat paper did because of the air that pushed up underneath it, slowing it down.

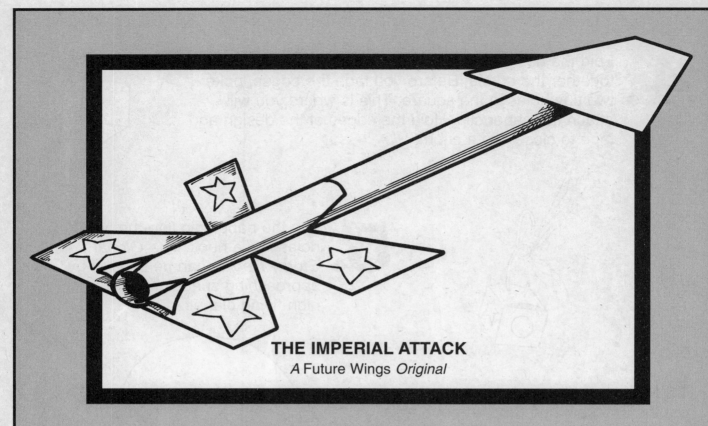

THE IMPERIAL ATTACK
A Future Wings Original

This megaspeed rocket was built to have an accuracy rate of 100 percent. Launched from a secret location, the *Imperial Attack* was designed to protect the skies above the White House. With a high-power laser beam, the rocket can lock instantly onto a suspicious image. Within a second it can tell if the object is friendly or hostile. Using specialized electronic vibrations, the rocket can seek and destroy a harmful object before it reaches its intended target.

YOU NEED:

three pieces of construction
   paper, 9″ x 8″, 4″ x 6″, and
   4″ x 4″
ruler
glue
four or five rubber bands

pencil
piece of tracing paper
scissors
tape
one or two jumbo paper clips
stars or stickers (optional)

1.

Lay the 9″ x 8″ paper flat in front of you. From the 9″ side, roll into a long tube. Opening should measure ¾″ wide. Glue along seams. Wrap four or five rubber bands around the tube until the glue is dry.

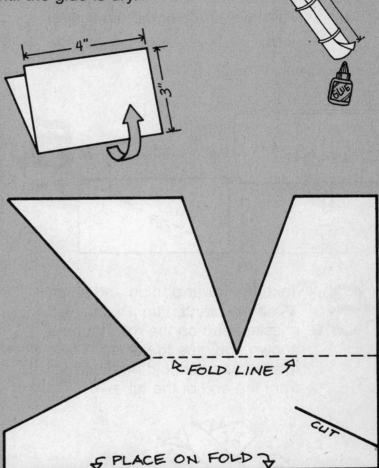

2.

Fold the 4″ x 6″ paper in half, keeping the fold along the bottom. Trace the actual-size wing design at the right onto a piece of tracing paper. Cut out and place over your folded paper, matching the bottom edges. Make sure to mark your dotted fold line and your 1″ cut line on the 4″ x 6″ paper design. Cut out the wing design and crease along the fold lines.

FOLD LINE

CUT

PLACE ON FOLD

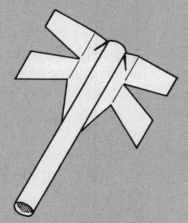

3.

Open wing up and place on the rolled tube as shown. Secure the center of the wings to tube with a thin line of glue.

4. Now bring each wing side together, closing around the tube. Gently press the wings out to each side and tape at seam. Turn over and spread out wings.

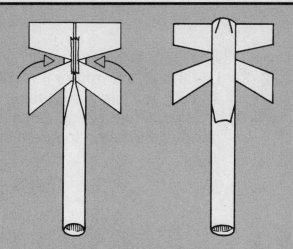

5. To make the missile head, fold the 4″ x 4″ paper in half. The fold will be on the bottom. Cut diagonally across the square from the bottom left to the top right corner.

CUT

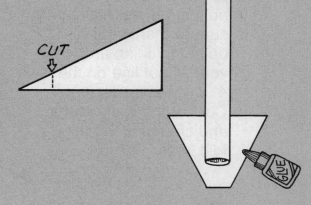

CUT

6. Take the lower portion and snip ¾″ off the pointed tip. Place the missile head on the rolled tube as shown and glue to secure. The missile head should be glued ¾″ from the end of the tube.

7. Turn over. Bend back side flaps outward. Use one or two jumbo paper clips under the nose for weight. Decorate if you wish, using stars or stickers.

TO FLY: Use the target thrust launch, with a hard and fast throw straight through the air.

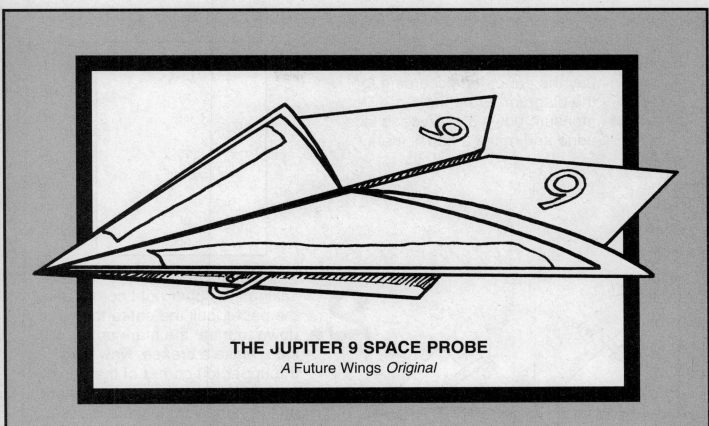

THE JUPITER 9 SPACE PROBE
A Future Wings *Original*

The *Jupiter 9 Space Probe* is powerful enough to send people to explore the outer atmosphere of Jupiter and its many moons. After blastoff, the three-person crew travels directly to the distant planet. Using computers on the *Space Probe*'s outside flaps, information is recorded about Jupiter's gases and temperatures. Four video cameras extend outward on command, recording the active volcanoes on Io, Jupiter's most unusual moon.

YOU NEED:

8½″ x 11″ piece of paper	scissors
ruler	two 4″ x 1″ pieces of foil
pencil	glue
small paper clip	stickers or markers (optional)

1. Lay the paper flat according to the diagram. From the top, measure down 8½" on each side edge and make a pencil mark.

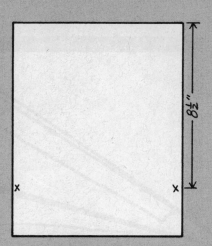

2. Taking the upper right corner of the paper, pull the entire top edge down to meet the mark on the left side. Make a crease. Now take the upper left corner of the paper and pull it down to meet the mark on the right side. Make a crease, creating a triangle sitting on top of a long rectangle.

3. Grasp the left side of the design and fold it to the right side. You will have a center flap showing between the two wings.

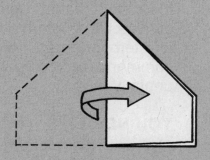

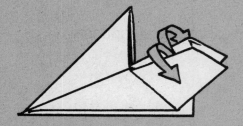

4. Turn the design so that the nose points to the left. Fold down the right and left wings at an angle, starting at the nose. Leave the middle flap standing straight up between the two wings.

5. To grasp the plane more easily, place the paper clip on the under edge about midway.

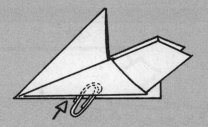

6. Cut the middle flap open by starting at the top point and working your way toward the nose. Open up the middle flaps to each side and crease.

7. Take the two pieces of foil and fold in half lengthwise. Glue to each outer side of the wings as shown. Decorate if you wish, using stickers or markers.

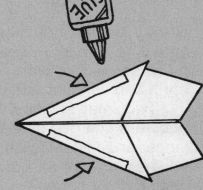

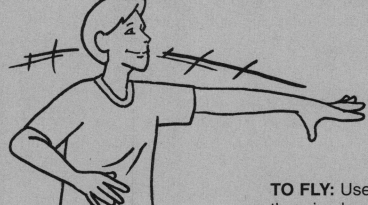

TO FLY: Use the straight pitch launch, throwing hard and fast.

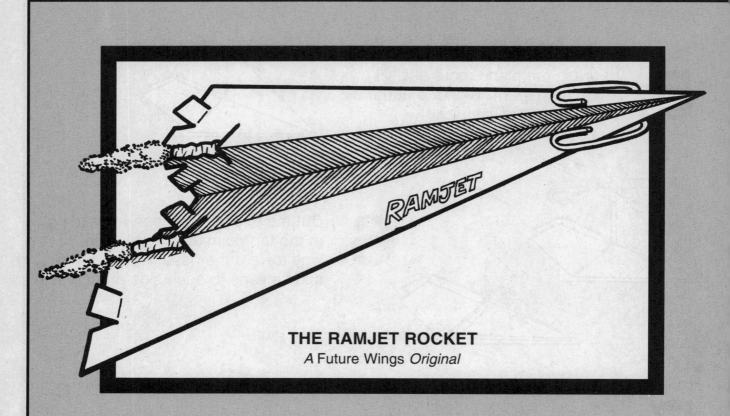

THE RAMJET ROCKET
A Future Wings *Original*

Rocket fuel engines burn strongly, but only for a short period of time. The *Ramjet Rocket* of the future runs on electric engines. It has an electronic pressure force that helps it to orbit the earth and conduct scientific experiments.

Two small engines, 9′ long, provide the power. Each engine is charged by electric heat so the rocket can travel longer and faster. Twice a day while in orbit, the electric engines burn for 2½ hours, supplying all the power the rocket needs for 24 hours.

YOU NEED:

8½″ x 11″ piece of construction paper	tape
scissors	paper clip
two cotton swabs	
two strips of foil	

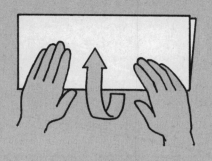

1. Fold the paper in half lengthwise. The fold should be on the bottom.

2. Fold down the top left corner as shown. Then flip over the paper so the folded corner is on the back side, to your right. Fold down the top right corner.

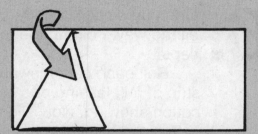

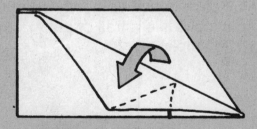

3. Fold down the right side wing starting at the nose point and working to the end, at an angle. Fold down the right side wing again, the same way.

4. Flip over and repeat with the left wing. Fold down starting at the nose point and working toward the end, at an angle. Fold again. When the wings are folded, it will look like a sleek dart.

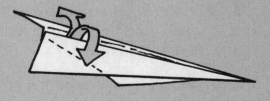

5. Turn so that the nose points to the left. Cut three slits, approximately 1″ each, as shown on the diagram's solid black lines. Make sure to keep the plane tightly folded so that you cut through both wings.

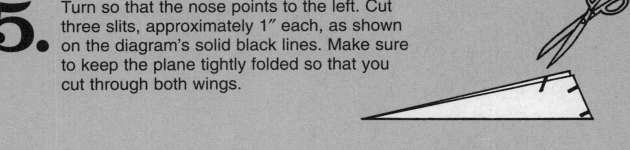

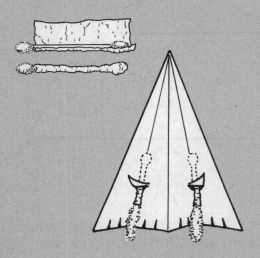

6. Open up design slightly, but not all the way. Fold up the four back flaps.

Roll each cotton swab in a strip of foil, leaving one end of cotton showing. Now slide each cotton swab into the top slit on each side of the plane and secure underneath with a piece of tape. Pull each cotton tip gently apart so it looks like a trail of puffy white smoke.

7. Attach the paper clip to the underside of the nose. Grasp two open flaps on the bottom together with your thumb and your two adjacent fingers.

TO FLY: Use a gentle straight pitch launch.

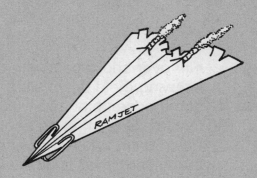

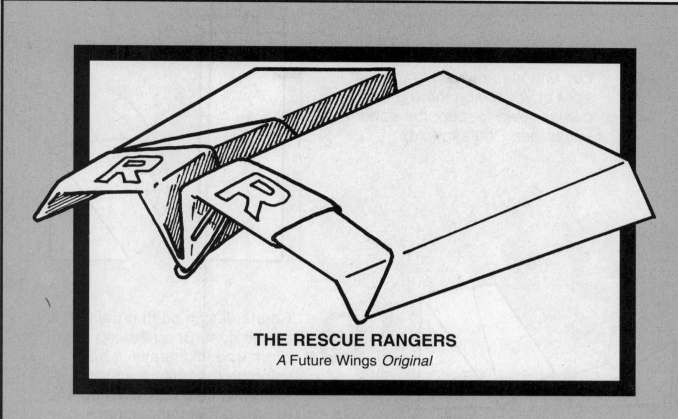

THE RESCUE RANGERS
A Future Wings *Original*

Traveling with lightning speed, the *Rescue Rangers* zoom through space toward a spaceship in trouble. Once the distress call comes in at the John F. Kennedy Space Center, the *Rangers* are ready for action. Each pilot is specially trained to repair such things as engine stalls and computer failures. Should a stalled craft resist repair, *Ranger 1* will stay with it while *Ranger 2* takes the astronauts back to earth quickly and safely.

YOU NEED:

two 3″ x 8½″ strips of black construction paper
ruler

pencil
two small paper clips
red marker

31

1. Lay one strip of black paper flat in front of you. Bring the top right corner down to meet the bottom left corner. Press to fold.

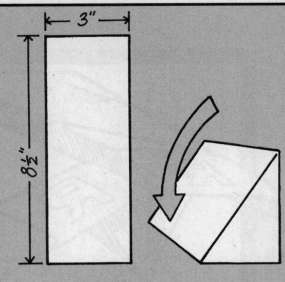

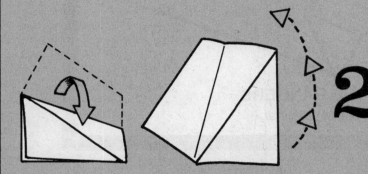

2. Rotate design so that the fold is on the right. Bring the top edge down and fold neatly in half, lining up the bottom edges evenly. Unfold this last step and rotate so that the original fold is now at the top.

3. Fold the top edge over ½", then fold the top edge over ½" again. Press the crease tightly.

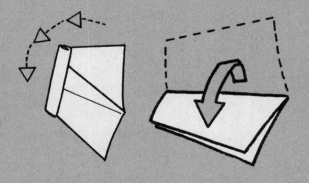

4. Turn so the new folds are on your left. Bring the top portion down and fold the design in half, lining up the bottom edges evenly.

5. Along the two bottom wing edges, sketch a line ¼" from the edge. Fold up on each line, making side flaps.

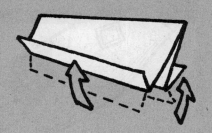

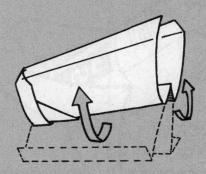

6. On each side of the top fold, sketch a line ¼" below it. Fold up the right and left sections, which are the wings, to the line you just made.

7. Turn the design, so the side flaps face downward. Attach one paper clip at the front nose section, which is the edge that has the folds. Using a red marker, print the letter **R** on each front side of the craft as shown. Follow the same instructions to make the second rescue rocket.

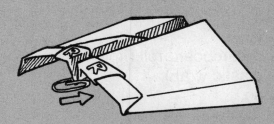

TO FLY: Use the straight pitch launch. Grasp the edge underneath the craft and toss out ahead of you.

AMAZING FACTOID!

Stuck in space? Not a problem. Backup manned rescue missions like those made by the *Rescue Rangers* are ready and available today for emergency recovery procedures. While they are not frequently used, they give astronauts a sense of comfort knowing they can be rescued millions of miles from the earth.

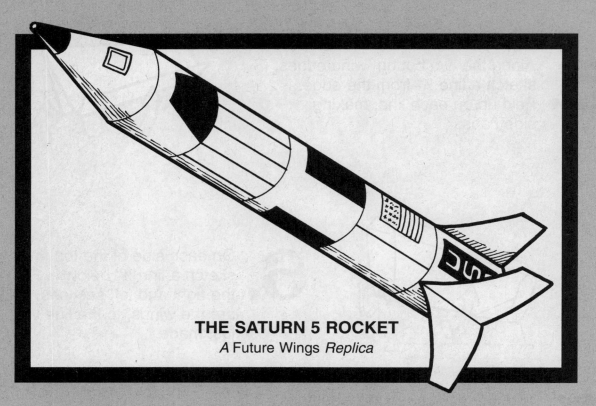

THE SATURN 5 ROCKET
A Future Wings *Replica*

It was July 16, 1969 . . . 4 . . . 3 . . . 2 . . . 1! As the launchpad countdown at the John F. Kennedy Space Center ended, the giant engines roared. The powerful *Saturn 5 Rocket* pushed upward, leaving behind a cloud of hot white flames and gas. The *Saturn 5* moon rocket had three steps to its launch. The first step was designed to lift the rocket off the ground. The second step sent the rocket into orbit. The third step carried the astronauts to the moon and back again. Weighing over 3,000 tons, the *Saturn 5 Rocket* brought man to the moon on July 20, 1969.

YOU NEED:

4 pieces of paper: one 6½″ x 11″ piece, one 7″ square, and two 5″ x 3″ pieces
ruler
black, red, and blue markers

12″ cardboard roll (from foil or plastic wrap)
tape
scissors
glue

1. Take the 6½″ x 11″ paper and measure across every 2″. At these marks, draw dark lines across the page with your black marker.

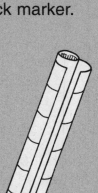

2. To make the body of the rocket, fit this paper around the cardboard roll. Secure along the seam with tape. The cardboard roll acts as a mold, which you will remove later.

3. To make the top portion, the Command Module, use your 7″ square of paper. Grasp opposite corners and, using your first two fingers, roll and shape the paper around your fingers to make a large cone shape with a pointed tip. Make sure to keep the bottom opening width about 2½″ so that it will slide easily over the top of the rocket.

CUT

4. Measure down 5″ from the point and cut across. Trim the bottom so that it is even, and then tuck under a ½″ seam all the way around.

5. Glue all the way around the top of the body. Now slide the module over the top of the rocket, overlapping it. Push down tightly and let the glue dry for five minutes.

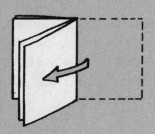

6. To make the bottom fins, take the two 5″ x 3″ pieces of paper. Place one on top of the other and fold in half widthwise. The fold should be on the right.

7. While still folded, measure down 2″ on the unfolded side (left). Cut diagonally up to the top right corner, discarding the small triangle pieces. Unfold. Take the two fins and secure them together with a small piece of tape at the top.

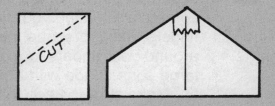

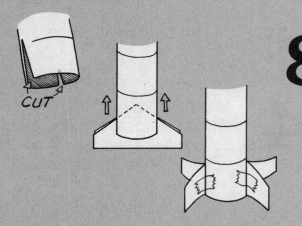

8. Gently slide cardboard mold out of rocket. On the body of the rocket, cut a 3″ slit going through both sides, from the bottom upward. Now slip the fins (point side first) into the 3″ slit at the bottom of the rocket.

Separate the fins and use tape on each side to hold in place.

9. Decorate with red and blue markers. You can follow the pattern at the left or design your own!

TO FLY: Using the target thrust launch, hold the rocket in the middle like a dart and throw hard and fast.

Fun Fact

What were the *Saturn 5* astronauts afraid would happen when they landed on the moon? That when they stepped down onto the moon, the moon dust would be so deep, they would sink!

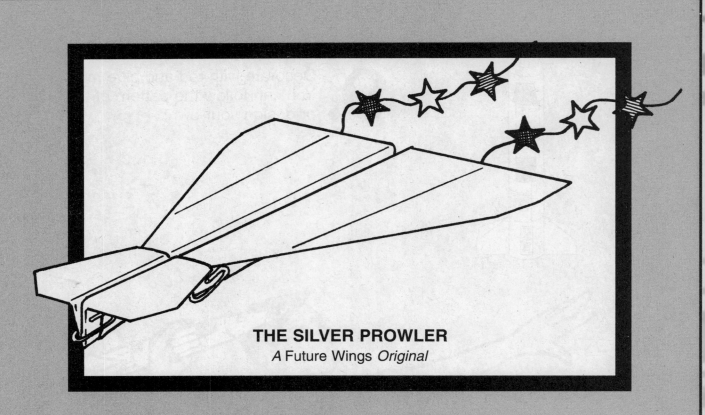

THE SILVER PROWLER
A Future Wings Original

The thick cloud cover and deep atmosphere of the planet Venus make it difficult to study from the earth. The *Silver Prowler* is designed to carry recording instruments to this distant planet.

After being launched from the earth, the *Silver Prowler* has four small engines outside the craft that blast gas into space to control the direction it travels. The on-craft astronauts study the radioactivity of rocks and take photographs of the rolling plains, mountains, and canyons that make up Venus's surface.

YOU NEED:

8½″ square of paper
pencil
ruler
two small paper clips

two 3½″ pieces of thread
six silver star stickers
tape

1. Fold the paper in half, then fold in half again. Open and lay it out in front of you as shown. Now fold the right and left top corners inward, lining them up with the middle crease.

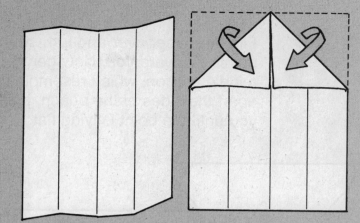

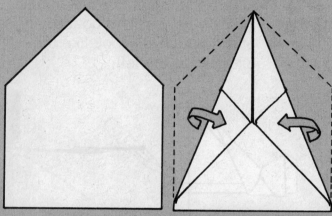

2. Flip the paper over. Fold the top right and left edges to the middle crease.

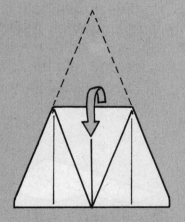

3. Flip the paper over again and fold the pointed nose down to the bottom edge.

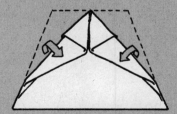

4. Flip the paper over and fold the top right and left edges to meet at the center as shown.

5. Flip the paper over and turn so that the nose is pointing toward you. Now gently pull open the middle section, which resembles a pouch. Pull apart the sides of the pouch, pulling down toward you until the point is lying flat.

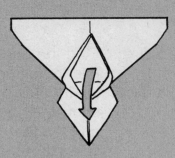

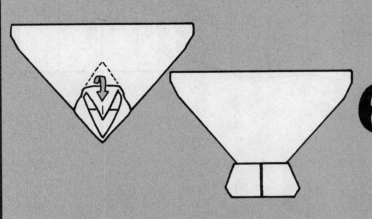

6. Lift up the point and tuck it back into the pouch. The bottom edges of the pouch will look like the diagram at the left.

7. Fold design in half, bringing the wings together. Sketch a ½″ line along the bottom edge on both sides and fold each wing out to this line, pressing hard to crease.

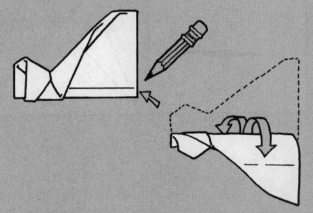

8. Slightly open the craft and attach two small paper clips along the bottom edge. One should be at the nose section, the other toward the middle section.

9. Take the two pieces of thread and place three silver star stickers on each. Take one end of each thread and tape to the back sections of the spacecraft.

TO FLY: Use the straight pitch launch, starting above your shoulders and tossing the craft upward and out.

40

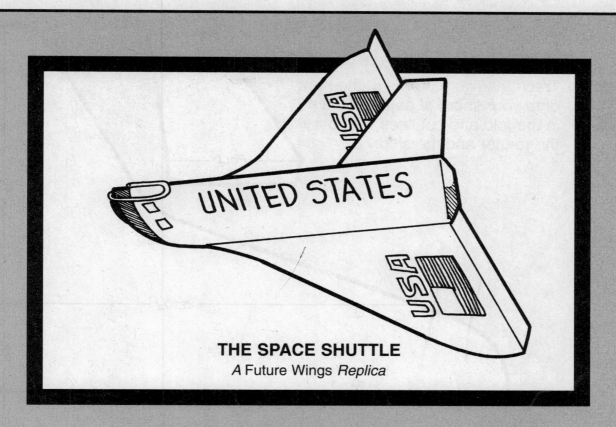

THE SPACE SHUTTLE
A Future Wings Replica

The *Space Shuttle* is a manned, reusable launch vehicle that orbits the earth and allows astronauts to conduct scientific experiments in space. The United States has four *Space Shuttles*, which are designed to carry up to 65,000 pounds and up to seven crew members and passengers. The shuttle is made up of three systems: the winged *Orbiter*, which carries the crew and cargo; the external fuel tanks; and the two solid rocket boosters, which lift the craft up into the atmosphere. Immediately after blastoff, the boosters parachute back into the ocean to be used again. The *Orbiter*, with its landing wheels down, glides back onto a runway at the end of its mission.

YOU NEED:

pencil	markers
8½″ x 11″ piece of paper	tape
scissors	small paper clip

1. Trace the two patterns at the right onto your sheet of paper. Sketch in the fold and cut lines. Cut out the rudder and the ship.

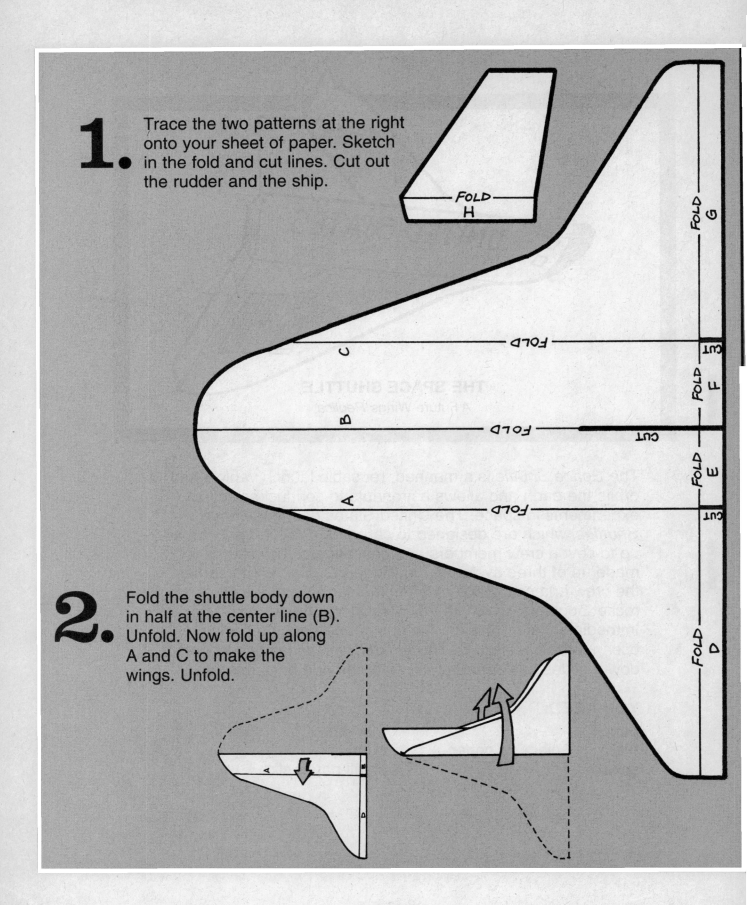

FOLD H

FOLD G

FOLD C

FOLD F

FOLD B

CUT

FOLD E

FOLD A

CUT

FOLD D

2. Fold the shuttle body down in half at the center line (B). Unfold. Now fold up along A and C to make the wings. Unfold.

3. Cut along the heavy solid lines. With the underside of the wings facing down, decorate with markers by drawing an American flag on each side below the letters **USA**. Or use your imagination!

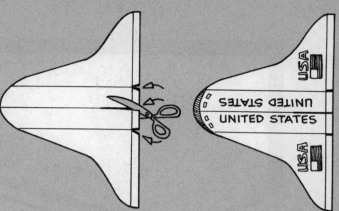

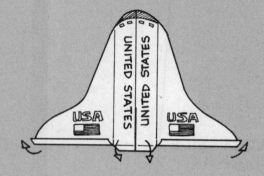

4. Place the shuttle flat in front of you. Fold the D and G flaps up. Fold the E and F flaps under.

5. Fold the rudder at the dotted line (H). Slide the rudder into the slit at the back end of the plane and tape to secure on the underside.

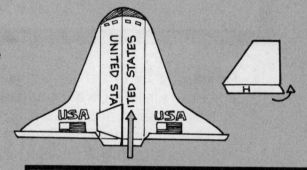

6. Use one paper clip at the center nose section.

TO FLY: Grasp the back end by using your thumb and next two fingers, with the fingers on top and thumb underneath. Hold the shuttle above your shoulder and toss out, using the straight pitch launch.

AMAZING FACTOID!

The four *Space Shuttles* were named for famous oceangoing ships: *Columbia, Challenger, Discovery,* and *Atlantis.* In 1991, the United States replaced the *Challenger* (which crashed in 1986) with the new *Endeavour.*

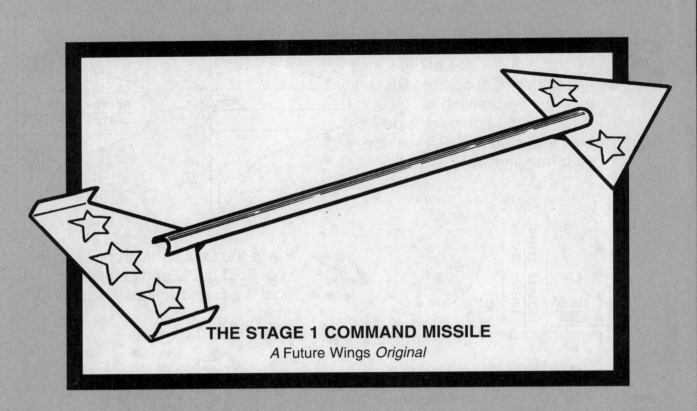

THE STAGE 1 COMMAND MISSILE
A Future Wings *Original*

Ready . . . aim . . . fire! The *Stage 1 Command Missile* is a powerful air-to-air weapon. It is fired from launches mounted on the wings of airplanes. Carrying a 100-pound explosive warhead, this missile is known for its quick reaction time and high acceleration. It travels 1,500 feet per second. The *Stage 1 Command Missile* is the best defense missile ever built to intercept approaching enemy aircraft.

YOU NEED:

drinking straw	pencil
scissors	scissors
ruler	tape
two pieces of paper, 3½" x 2" and 2½" x 1½"	red and blue stars

1. At each end of the straw, cut a 1" slit.

2. Fold your 3½" x 2" paper in half widthwise. The fold should be on your right. Measure 1" down on the left (unfolded) edge and make a pencil mark. Make a cut through both sides up to the top right corner. Open up design.

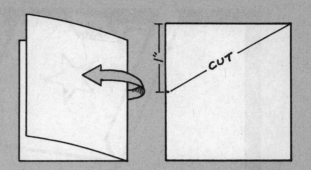

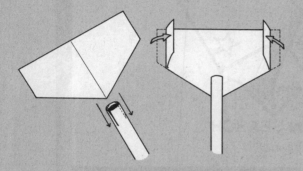

3. Slide the middle point into the slit at one end of the straw. Use a small piece of tape to hold in place. Turn up both back sides ½" as shown.

4. Take the 2½" x 1½" piece of paper and make a mark along the top edge, exactly halfway. From this point, draw two lines down to each bottom corner to make a triangle shape. Cut out the triangle.

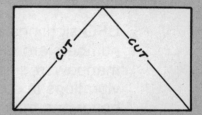

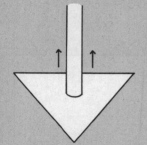

5. Slide the triangle, the missile head, into the other end of the straw so that the center point is facing away from the rest of the missile. Secure with a small piece of tape. Decorate with red and blue stars.

TO FLY: Use the target thrust launch. Hold the missile above your head, aim at a target, and throw hard and fast.

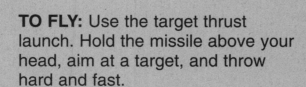

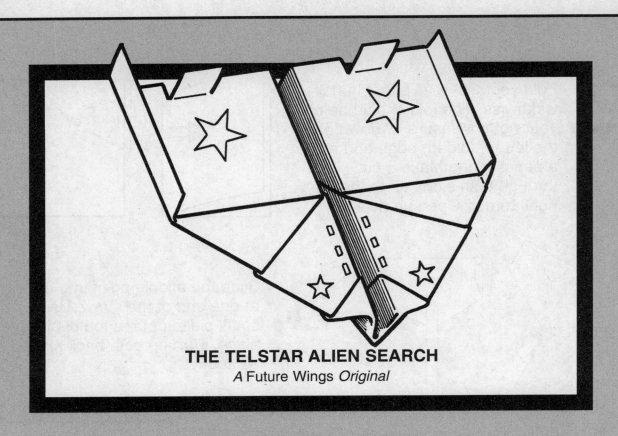

THE TELSTAR ALIEN SEARCH
A Future Wings *Original*

UFO sightings and encounters are occurring in increasing numbers around the world. The *Telstar Alien Search* is a manpowered spacecraft designed to detect sounds and vibrations in space that don't come from the earth. It is able to hover and make 90-degree turns at high speeds. The *Telstar Alien Search* can detect UFOs that mysteriously disappear from sight and from ground radar stations.

YOU NEED:
8½" x 11" sheet of paper   scissors
ruler   markers
pencil

1. Lay out your paper on a flat surface. Measure down 8½" on the right edge. Mark this spot with your pencil. Now measure down 8½" on the left edge. Make another small mark.

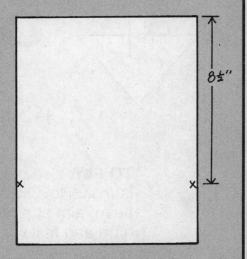

2.

Fold the top left corner down to meet the mark at the right edge. Crease. Fold the top right corner down to meet the mark at the left edge. Crease. You will have formed a large triangle shape at the top of the paper.

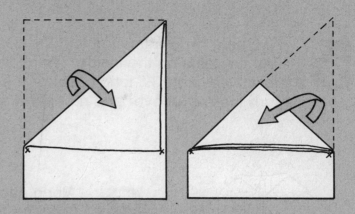

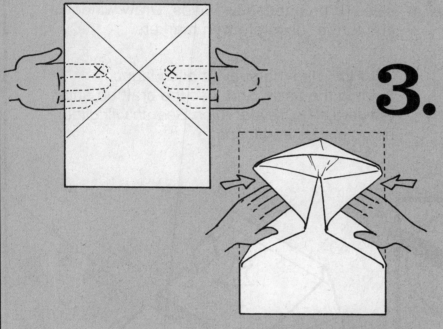

3.

Now open up the creases and lay the paper flat. Make two **X** marks on either side of the paper as shown in the diagram. Placing your hands behind the paper at the two **X** spots, squash the two sides inward to meet at the center fold.

4.

Flatten out this shape into a 3-D triangle. Now take each corner of the triangle and bring it up to meet at the top point of the paper. Press to crease. Fold top point down 1".

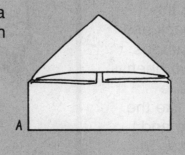

A

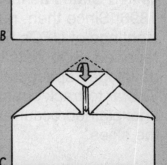

B

C

5. To create two wings, first fold the design in half with the folds on the inside. Then fold one wing down, leaving a ½"-long base for the spacecraft. Turn the rocket over and repeat for second wing.

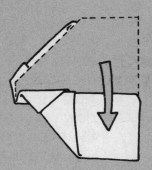

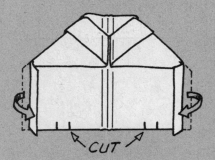

CUT

6. Along each side of the aircraft, fold up a ½" flap. Cut two slits, ¼" each, at the back of each side. Turn up these two flaps. Draw windows and further decorate with markers.

TO FLY: Use the straight pitch launch, holding the base, and toss the craft up and outward. The *Telstar Alien Search* will glide, doing circles and loops.

AMAZING FACTOID!

"Mystery ships" were reported being seen flying over the United States as far back as 1896! Since then, numerous sightings of UFOs have been reported. Scientists have developed spacecraft like the *Telstar* to track strange and unexplained occurrences in the skies.

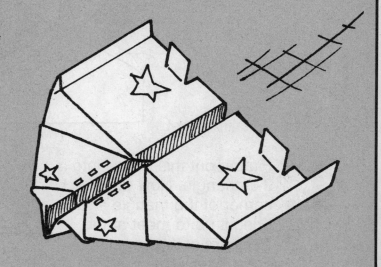

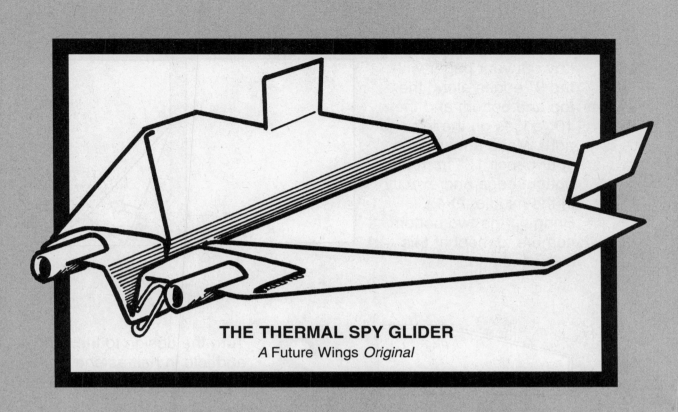

THE THERMAL SPY GLIDER
A Future Wings *Original*

Built for the 21st century, the *Thermal Spy Glider* is able to climb and dive with the use of air currents. Dropped from a hovering spaceship, this aircraft can secretly detect missile sights on the ground in countries all over the world.

Without an engine, it silently swoops through warm air currents called thermals. At the top of one thermal the pilot finds and reaches another thermal before dropping too far. The *Spy Glider* is able to travel hundreds of miles on a warm day, bringing back top-secret information from photographs taken by its two front-mounted cameras.

YOU NEED:
10" x 9" piece of construction
  paper
pencil
ruler
scissors

two 1" drinking straw pieces
two jumbo paper clips
tape
markers or stickers (optional)

1. Lay out your paper with the 9″ edges along the top and bottom and the 10″ edges on the left and right. Make a mark with your pencil 1½″ from the bottom edge and exactly in the middle, at 4½″. Bring up the two bottom corners to meet at this mark and fold.

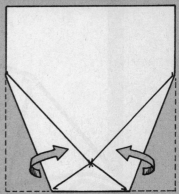

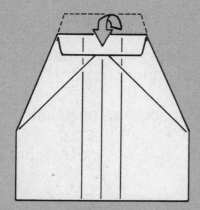

2. Turn the design to the side and fold in half as shown.

3. Lightly sketch a 1″ line along the bottom edge of the glider and fold the wing along it. Turn over and repeat for the other wing.

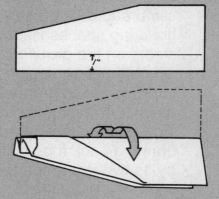

4. Flatten out the wings. Fold up the front nose edge 1″ and crease.

5. Gently crease the center line to create a small dip between the wings. To make the two cameras, cut a slit halfway into each straw piece, lengthwise. Slide the cut side over the front edge of the glider on each side as shown. Cameras should be positioned 1″ from each side's edge.

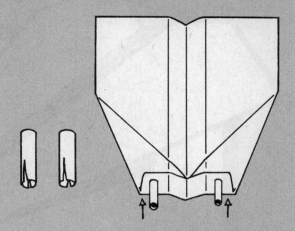

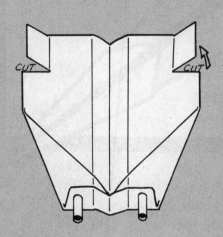

6. Make a mark 2″ from each back edge. Cut in 1″ as shown and turn flaps up slightly.

7. Attach two jumbo paper clips underneath toward front nose section. Decorate with markers or stickers if desired.

TO FLY: Toss gently upward and out using the straight pitch launch.

Fun Fact

The *Thermal Spy Glider* is modeled after today's gliders that are used all over the world. They stay up in the air the same way that birds do, floating upward on rising currents of warm air.

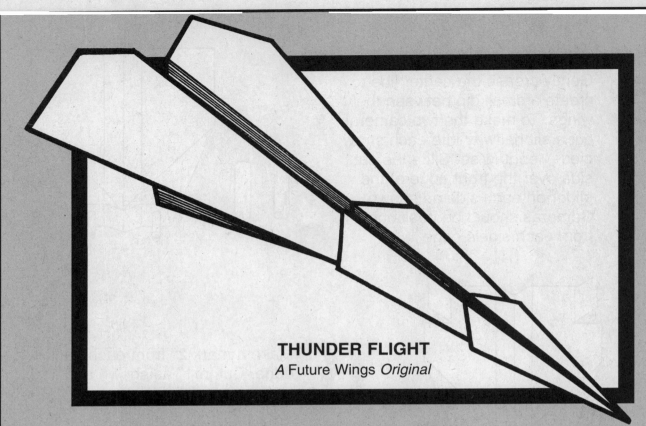

THUNDER FLIGHT
A Future Wings *Original*

In flight, it rumbles noisily like loud thunder. Over 50 feet in length and weighing 2,000 pounds, this awesome rocket studies the atmosphere 100 miles above the earth. This altitude is too thin to support air balloons and too dense for orbiting satellites. *Thunder Flight* breaks into three smaller rockets to carry out important space science research. It then rejoins before returning to the earth by parachute.

YOU NEED:
3 pieces of paper: one 8½" x 11", one 4½" x 7", and one 4" x 2½"

tape
markers or crayons (optional)

1. Fold the 8½" x 11" paper in half widthwise. Open and lay flat horizontally. Fold down the right and left top corners to the middle crease.

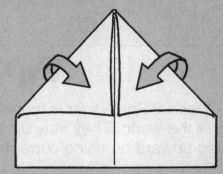

2. Bring in the top right and left edges again to the middle crease as shown.

Fold the left side of the plane to meet the right side.

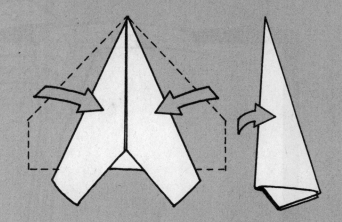

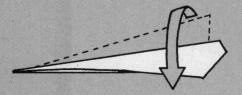

3. Turn the nose point to the left. From the nose point to the wing tip, fold the right and left wings down, aligning the bottom edges.

4. Follow the same directions for Steps 1 through 3 using the other two pieces of paper for the smaller rockets.

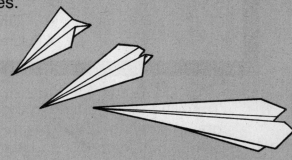

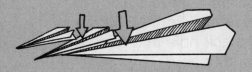

5. Slide the middle-sized plane into the top fold of the largest plane, overlapping about a third of itself over the main craft. Then add the smallest plane at the front nose section, again overlapping itself over the middle plane.

6. Tape the smaller planes to the large one along the top center crease. Flip over and secure again with tape along the back center seam. Decorate with markers or crayons if desired.

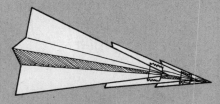

TO FLY: Grasp the back of the plane at the middle, using your thumb underneath and forefinger on top. Use the straight pitch launch, tossing upward and out.

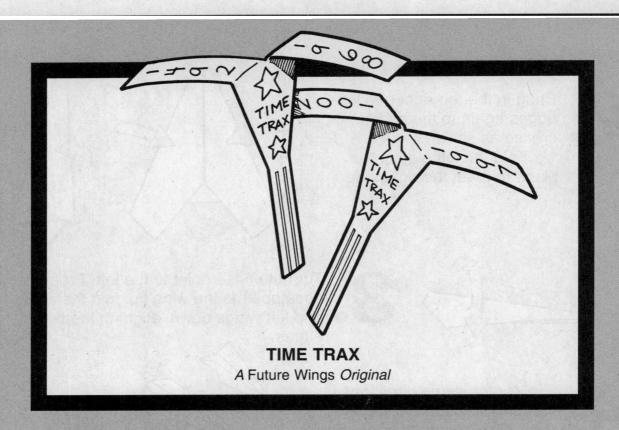

TIME TRAX
A Future Wings *Original*

Traveling through time in the year 2050 is now possible with the gravity-defying *Time Trax* machine. Guided by only a pair of spinning blades, this spaceship flies faster than the speed of light.

Time Trax whirls through the galaxies toward a large black hole deep in space, held open by a powerful energy force field. To get to other universes, *Time Trax* enters the black hole and finds it has arrived in a different dimension of time and space.

YOU NEED:

2″ x 9″ piece of colored construction paper
pencil
ruler

scissors
tape
black marker

1. Lay the paper vertically in front of you. Along the left edge from the top, make a pencil mark at 3″. Measure down 3″ more and make a second mark.

2. Using these marks as guidelines, copy the broken and solid lines on your design as shown in the diagram at right.

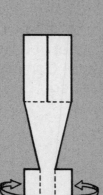

3. Cut on the solid lines and fold back on the lower broken lines.

4. Flip the design over and use a small piece of tape to secure the back seam at the stem. Turn the bottom of the stem up approximately ½″ and hold in place with a small piece of tape.

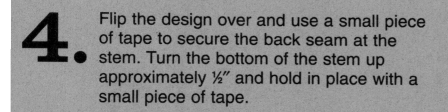

AMAZING FACTOID! Is time travel possible? Could you really go back to the Middle Ages or zoom ahead to the 23rd century? Although this may sound like science fiction, time travel is taken seriously and is being researched by many scientists and astronomers. Experts believe that the way to accomplish this is by diving into a powerful force field in space called a black hole and emerging in another place and time. In the 1970s, astronomers discovered what seem to be real black holes in our own Milky Way galaxy and in the heart of other galaxies.

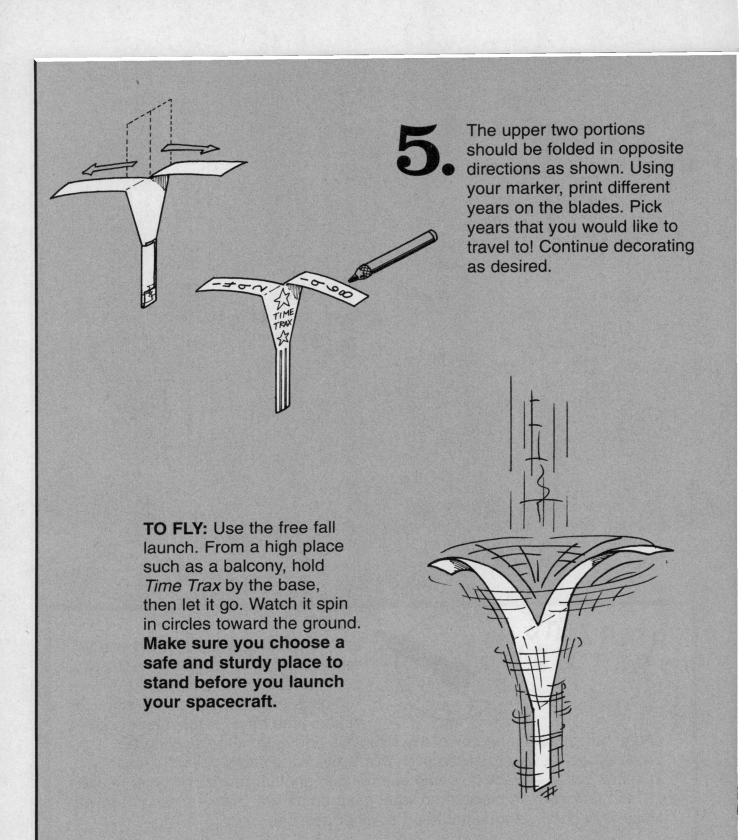

5. The upper two portions should be folded in opposite directions as shown. Using your marker, print different years on the blades. Pick years that you would like to travel to! Continue decorating as desired.

TO FLY: Use the free fall launch. From a high place such as a balcony, hold *Time Trax* by the base, then let it go. Watch it spin in circles toward the ground. **Make sure you choose a safe and sturdy place to stand before you launch your spacecraft.**

THE ULYSSES SOLAR SATELLITE
A Future Wings *Replica*

At 814 pounds, the *Ulysses Solar Satellite* was designed to fly over the sun and gather information to share with countries around the world. Launched from the space shuttle *Discovery* in October 1990, the satellite studied the solar winds and radiation, as well as the strange occurrences near the sun's north and south poles, which have never been examined by spacecraft. It continued to send back information using computers and completed its mission in October 1995, five years after its launch.

YOU NEED:
7" paper plate   tape
foil   stickers
three toothpicks

1. Completely wrap the bottom side of the paper plate with a sheet of foil. Be sure to wrap the foil around the edges.

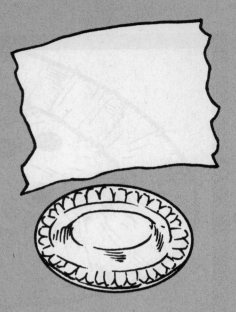

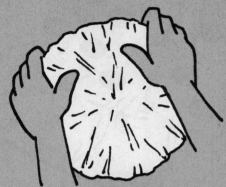

2. To make the X-ray detectors that lock onto bursts of cosmic energy, line up the three toothpicks. Secure together at one end with tape. Wrap a small piece of foil around the tape.

3. Carefully punch the sharp ends of the toothpicks into the middle of the plate (foil side). The loose ends of the toothpicks should be placed approximately ½″ apart from each other.

4. Decorate with colorful stickers over the foil.

TO FLY: Use the disc launch, holding the side of the plate and tossing it out into the air like a Frisbee®.

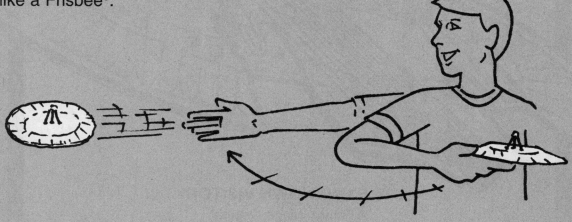

Does the sun constantly change? To people on the earth, it always appears the same, shining bright and steady in the sky. But when it is observed with special equipment like that of the *Ulysses,* many changes in the sun are visible. It looks like it is moving in slow motion, bubbling and boiling. Scientists compare this movement to rice boiling in water.

When rice boils, tiny pieces quickly appear and then disappear and others take their place. This is what the sun's surface really looks like, although the changes take several minutes to occur.

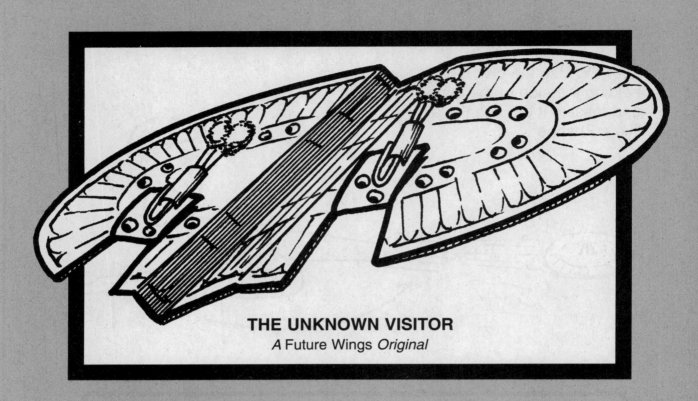

THE UNKNOWN VISITOR
A Future Wings *Original*

For years, mysterious spaceship sightings have been reported in places all over the world. Some people have described seeing a disk-shaped spacecraft approximately 100 feet across that moves and turns at incredible speeds and has eyes that dart about in all directions. The *Unknown Visitor* is said to appear briefly in the sky, observe, and then move off, disappearing in a trail of pulsating light.

YOU NEED:

paper plate
ruler
pencil
scissors
two jumbo paper clips

tape
two 1½" drinking straw pieces
two cotton swabs
black marker

1. Fold the paper plate in half. The ridges or design should be on the inside.

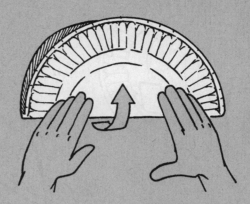

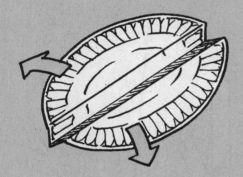

2. On each side, measure out ½" from the fold, then lightly draw a line along this mark. Now fold each side down along these sketched lines to create wings.

3. At the front edge, measure 1½" from each side of the center crease. Starting there, cut two 1"-long lines on each side as shown. Lines should be 1" apart from each other.

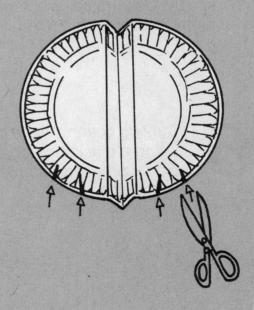

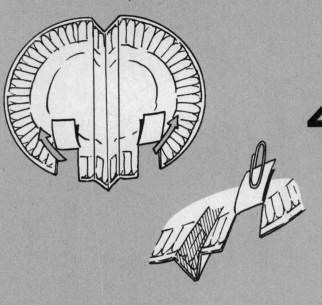

4. Lift up the front flaps and attach a jumbo paper clip to the top of each flap. Place a 2″ piece of tape on the back of each flap, securing it to the base.

5. Taking the two straw pieces, from the bottom, cut a slit halfway into each straw through both sides. Now slide each straw (cut-side first) onto the paper clip and push it down until it fits snugly. Use a small piece of tape to secure the straw.

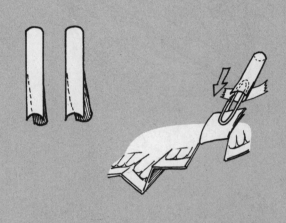

6. Cut two cotton swabs in half. Using a black marker, color big round eyeballs on all four cotton tips.

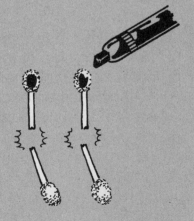

7. Slide two cotton swabs into each straw at the top and push down until they fit snugly. Position one slightly higher than the other.

8. Using your black marker, decorate your spaceship with more eyes looking in different directions.

TO FLY: Grasp the underside of the craft in the middle. Hold above your shoulder and toss out gently in a straight pitch launch for a smooth glide.

Fun Fact

Are we being watched? Mysterious sightings are being taken more seriously now than ever before. With recent photographs and discoveries of oxygen and water brought back from other planets, some scientists feel that life could exist elsewhere in the universe. Who knows—maybe there's an *Unknown Visitor* coming to a landing strip near you!

Glossary

asteroid: A small starlike or planetlike object that revolves around the sun, mostly between the orbits of Mars and Jupiter.

atmosphere: 1) The blanket of air or gas surrounding a planet; 2) The air surrounding the earth, in which we live and fly.

gravity: The force that makes objects fall down toward the center of the earth and keeps them from flying off into space.

meteor: A small piece of matter in space that is visible when it enters the earth's atmosphere.

meteorite: The part of a meteor that reaches the earth's surface before being vaporized.

meteoroid: Fragments of matter that orbit the sun and enter the earth's atmosphere to form meteors.

Milky Way galaxy: The sun and planets in the solar system, which includes billions of stars.

NASA: The National Aeronautics and Space Administration, the organization in charge of space exploration on behalf of the United States.

orbit: The path taken by one object or planet circling around another one, as the earth does around the sun.

radar: A device or system that uses a radio transmitter and a receiver. It produces radio waves that can detect the position of things in the distance and the direction of moving objects.

rocket: A missile or jet engine that is driven through the air by the reaction of escaping gases.

satellite (artificial): An unmanned, man-made vehicle sent out into orbit from the earth to collect scientific information.

solar system: The sun and its family of orbiting planets, asteroids, meteoroids, and comets.

space probe: An unmanned spacecraft, such as the *Viking* and the *Voyager,* sent to gather information about other planets and stars in the solar system.

space shuttle: A reusable spacecraft designed to transport people and cargo between the earth and space.

space station: A manned spacecraft that orbits the earth and on which crew members can live and work for long periods of time.